Usborne Workbooks

Times Tables

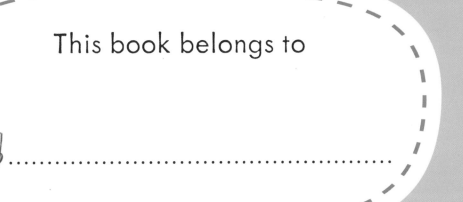

This book belongs to

....

There are answers on page 27, and notes
for grown-ups at the back of the book.

Here are some of the animals you will meet in this book.
They are learning the 7, 9, 11 and 12 times tables.

You can use a pen or pencil to help the animals with all the times tables questions
in this book. Draw over the dotted lines and write the numbers in the boxes.

Usborne Workbooks
Times Tables

Illustrated by Elisa Paganelli

Written by Holly Bathie
Designed by Maddison Warnes

Zeb

Wolfy

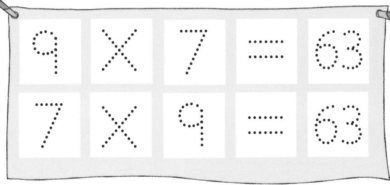

$$9 \times 7 = 63$$
$$7 \times 9 = 63$$

At the end of the book there are blank pages for more times tables practice.

Pat

Edited by Jessica Greenwell
and Kristie Pickersgill
Series Editor: Felicity Brooks

Times tables reminder

Each of these bugs has 3 spots. Pat has written in the boxes how many bugs are on each leaf. Use the 3 times table to find the total number of spots on each leaf without counting.

These pages will help you to remember the 3, 4, 6 and 8 times tables.

Pat

 ☐ x 6 = ☐

 ☐ x 3 = ☐

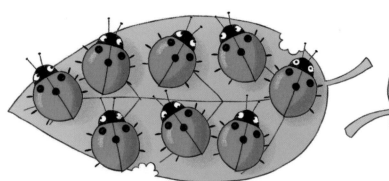

☐ x 8 = ☐

 ☐ x 7 = ☐

Check you can remember the 6 times table by doubling the number of spots on each bug. You could draw more spots to help you. Then complete the calculations below.

☐ x 6 = ☐

☐ x 8 = ☐

☐ x 3 = ☐

☐ x 7 = ☐

Help Gloria with her calculations to see if you can remember the 4 times table.

Every butterfly has 4 spots. Use the 4 times table to find the total number of spots in each group without counting.

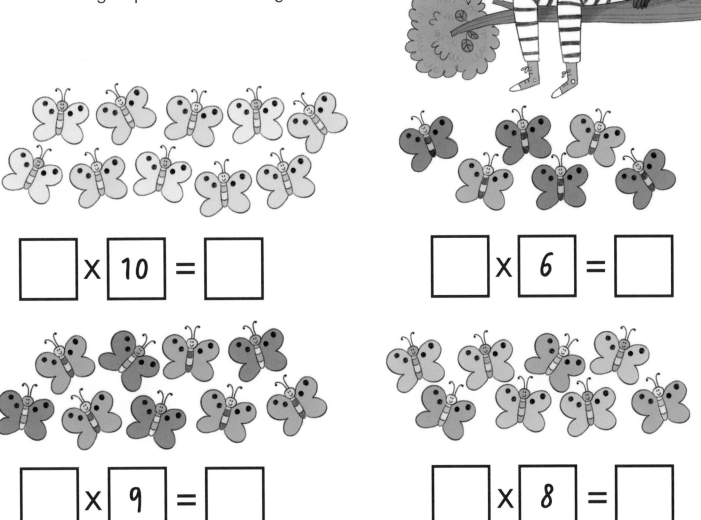

I've written the number of butterflies in each group for you.

Gloria

☐ X 10 = ☐

☐ X 6 = ☐

☐ X 9 = ☐

☐ X 8 = ☐

Check you can remember the 8 times table by doubling the spots on each butterfly.
You could draw more spots to help you. Complete the calculations below.

☐ X 10 = ☐

☐ X 9 = ☐

☐ X 6 = ☐

☐ X 8 = ☐

Groups of 7

Ping is fishing at an ice hole and wants to work out how many fish there are in the water. Draw a ring around 7 fish, then draw a ring around another group of 7. Keep going until all the fish are in groups of 7.

Plenty of fish today!

Ping

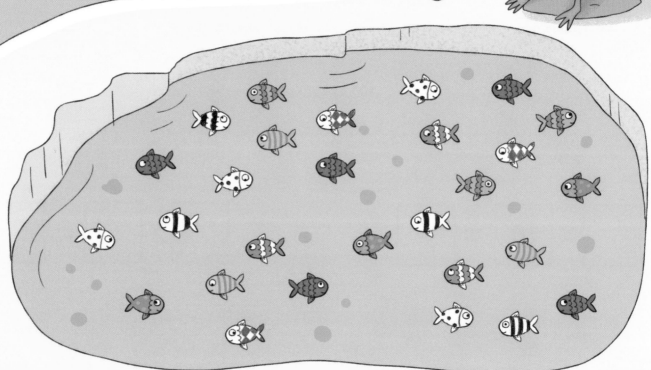

Count how many groups you have made, then complete this calculation.

 X =

Do you already know these calculations from other times tables?

If there were double the number of groups, how many fish would there be? Complete this calculation to find out.

 X =

The 7 times table

Can you help the penguins complete this times table? You may know some of the calculations from other tables.

I know the 2, 5 and 10 times tables, so I can fill in those answers.

I know the 3, 4, 6 and 8 times tables, so I can fill those in.

Now we just need to add or subtract 7 to fill in any gaps in the table.

You could use the number line at the bottom of the page to help you.

1 X 7 =

2 X 7 =

3 X 7 =

4 X 7 =

5 X 7 =

6 X 7 =

7 X 7 =

8 X 7 =

9 X 7 =

10 X 7 =

Subtract 7

Add 7

42   49   56   63   70

Groups of 9

Bruce is busy in the sweetshop putting out all the sweets in trays of 9. Help the mice complete the labels for him.

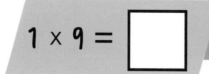 I've got 1 row of 9 lemon drops.

$1 \times 9 = \boxed{}$

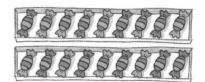

$2 \times 9 = \boxed{}$

Phew! Lots to count.

$3 \times 9 = \boxed{}$

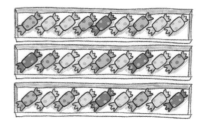

These sweets aren't ready yet. Can we still finish the label?

 Ummmm...

$4 \times 9 = \boxed{}$

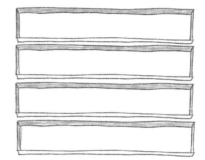

 Yes, we can do it. The answer will be 9 more than the last label.

 So let's count in 9s: 9, 18, 27...

 I wonder if there's an easier way...

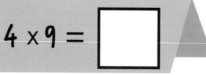

Bruce knows the 10 times table and thinks he could help the mice.

Pin, let's put out **4** more sweets – **1** more for each tray. Then we'll have **4** trays of **10** instead. That would be easier.

4 lots of **10** is **40**.

But there's no room for another sweet on each tray, Bruce.

Ok, I'll take these **4** sweets away then. **40** take away **4** is **36**.

Oh, that must be the answer! **4** lots of **9** is **36**.

Pin

Hooray!

Can you complete the next label, using the 10 times table to help you? The numbers in the blue boxes will be the same.

$$5 \times 10 = \boxed{}$$

$$\boxed{} - 5 = \boxed{}$$

$$5 \times 9 = \boxed{}$$

Write another 9 times table calculation here, using the 10 times table to help you.

Don't forget to subtract after you have multiplied by **10**.

$$\boxed{} \times \boxed{9} = \boxed{}$$

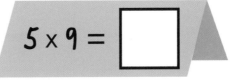

Try writing some more 9 times table calculations on page 28. You could use the 10 times table to help you.

Groups of 11

The mice are making bunting for the fair and want to put 11 paper flags on each string. They have put 10 on each string so far. Complete their 10 times table calculations.

Hold tight!

1 x ☐ = ☐

2 x ☐ = ☐

3 x ☐ = ☐

Now draw 1 more flag on each string, for the mice, and complete the 11 times table calculations below.

1 x ☐ = ☐   2 x ☐ = ☐   3 x ☐ = ☐

Have you noticed a pattern? Complete these 11 times table calculations. You could draw strings of flags above to help you.

4 × ☐ = ☐

5 × ☐ = ☐

Write another 11 times table calculation below.

☐ × ☐ = ☐

POP!

Ooops!

If you want to try the 12 times table, you could draw another flag on each string on the opposite page, then complete the calculations below.

1 × ☐ = ☐   2 × ☐ = ☐   3 × ☐ = ☐

The 9 and 11 times tables

Hop and Zeb are spotting patterns in this number grid. Hop has circled the first few numbers in the 9 times table. Can you circle the rest?

I've counted 9 three times to get to 27. 3 lots of 9 is 27.

Draw a triangle around each of the numbers in the 11 times table for me, please.

1	2	3	4	5	6	7	8	(9)	10
11	12	13	14	15	16	17	(18)	19	20
21	22	23	24	25	26	(27)	28	29	30
31	32	33	34	35	36	37	38	39	40
41	42	43	44	45	46	47	48	49	50
51	52	53	54	55	56	57	58	59	60
61	62	63	64	65	66	67	68	69	70
71	72	73	74	75	76	77	78	79	80
81	82	83	84	85	86	87	88	89	90
91	92	93	94	95	96	97	98	99	100
101	102	103	104	105	106	107	108	109	110

Which number is in both the 9 times table and the 11 times table? Write it in this box.

Help Kat complete these times tables.

The 9 times table

1	×	9	=
2	×	9	=
3	×	9	=
4	×	9	=
5	×	9	=
6	×	9	=
7	×	9	=
8	×	9	=
9	×	9	=
10	×	9	=

The 11 times table

1	×	11	=
2	×	11	=
3	×	11	=
4	×	11	=
5	×	11	=
6	×	11	=
7	×	11	=
8	×	11	=
9	×	11	=
10	×	11	=

Can you see any patterns?

No, it's too dark down here!

Word problems for 9 and 11

Wolfy, Bruce and Hop are growing flowers in the garden.
Write a multiplying calculation to answer each animal's question.

I'm going to plant **4** rows of **9** poppies. How many poppies will there be altogether?

Wolfy

☐ X ☐ = ☐

My full watering can holds enough water for **8** flowers. If I filled it **11** times, how many flowers could I water?

☐ X ☐ = ☐

☐ X ☐ = ☐

Each of my flowers has **10** petals. How many petals are there altogether?

9   18   27   36   45   54   63   72   81   90

Pin, Gloria and Kat are growing vegetables.
Write a multiplying calculation to answer
each animal's question.

Each pea pod has 11 peas inside. How many peas are there altogether?

□ X □ = □

I have sown 9 carrot seeds in each row. How many seeds have I sown altogether?

□ X □ = □

□ X □ = □

How many peppers will there be if 9 grow on each plant?

11   22   33   44   55   66   77   88   99   110

The 12 times table

Count along the number grid in 12s and draw a circle around each number in the 12 times table.

The 12 times table goes past 100!

Add more numbers to the bottom part of the grid to continue the pattern up to 12 lots of 12.

1	2	3	4	5	6	7	8	9	10
11	12	13	14	15	16	17	18	19	20
21	22	23	24	25	26	27	28	29	30
31	32	33	34	35	36	37	38	39	40
41	42	43	44	45	46	47	48	49	50
51	52	53	54	55	56	57	58	59	60
61	62	63	64	65	66	67	68	69	70
71	72	73	74	75	76	77	78	79	80
81	82	83	84	85	86	87	88	89	90
91	92	93	94	95	96	97	98	99	100

12   24   36   48   60   72

Now that you have finished the grid, complete the 12 times table.

To check your answers, remember **12** is double **6**, so you can double all the numbers in the 6 times table to get the 12 times table.

1 x 6 = 6
2 x 6 = 12
3 x 6 = 18
4 x 6 = 24
5 x 6 = 30
6 x 6 = 36
7 x 6 = 42
8 x 6 = 48
9 x 6 = 54
10 x 6 = 60

Hurry up, Bruce!

Check the answers on page 27 to see if you are right.

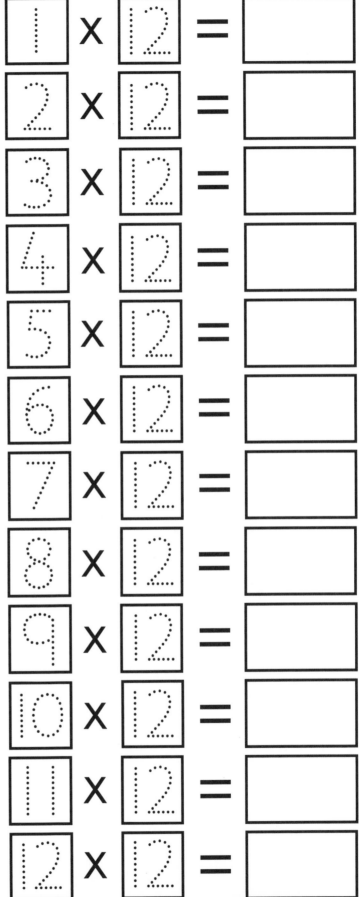

1 X 12 =

2 X 12 =

3 X 12 =

4 X 12 =

5 X 12 =

6 X 12 =

7 X 12 =

8 X 12 =

9 X 12 =

10 X 12 =

11 X 12 =

12 X 12 =

84   96   108   120   132   144

Word problems for 7 and 12

The animals are off on holiday. Write a multiplying calculation to answer each of their questions.

$\square \times \square = \square$

We each have 5 bags. How many bags are there altogether?

The bus has 2 decks and 12 seats on each deck. How many seats are there altogether?

$\square \times \square = \square$

Beep Beep!

There's space for 3 animals in each car. How many animals could travel by car altogether?

$\square \times \square = \square$

| 7 | 14 | 21 | 28 | 35 | 42 | 49 | 56 | 63 | 70 |

The boat waits for 6 minutes at each stop and there are 12 stops. How many minutes will it wait for altogether?

☐ ✕ ☐ = ☐

☐ ✕ ☐ = ☐

My plane has 12 rows of 10 seats. How many seats are there altogether?

☐ ✕ ☐ = ☐

My train has 7 carriages and each carriage has 7 seats. How many seats are there altogether?

12   24   36   48   60   72   84   96   108   120

Multiplication square

This multiplication square lists all the tables vertically, in columns. The tables are also listed horizontally, in rows.

The 2 times table is down this column.

The 10 times table is down this column.

The 2 times table is along this row, too.

x	1	2	3	4	5	6	7	8	9	10	11	12
1	1	2	3	4	5	6	7	8	9	10	11	12
2	2	4	6	8	10	12	14	16	18	20	22	24
3	3	6	9	12	15	18	21	24	27	30	33	36
4	4	8	12	16	20	24	28	32	36	40	44	48
5	5	10	15	20	25	30	35	40	45	50	55	60
6	6	12	18	24	30	36	42	48	54	60	66	72
7	7	14	21	28	35	42	49	56	63	70	77	84
8	8	16	24	32	40	48	56	64	72	80	88	96
9	9	18	27	36	45	54	63	72	81	90	99	108
10	10	20	30	40	50	60	70	80	90	100	110	120
11	11	22	33	44	55	66	77	88	99	110	121	132
12	12	24	36	48	60	72	84	96	108	120	132	144

Can you find the 10 times table row that matches Pin's 10 times table column? Try finding the matching row for each of the other columns, too.

Choose a number from the yellow row along the top of the square, and a number from the green column down the side, to multiply together. Write them in the boxes below.

[ ] X [ ] = [ ]

Run one finger down the column of the yellow number and another along the row of the green number. The answer is where your fingers meet. Complete the calculation.

Choose different pairs of yellow and green numbers and write multiplying calculations for them in the boxes below.

[ ] X [ ] = [ ]

[ ] X [ ] = [ ]

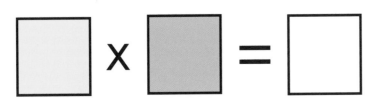

This square is really useful.

Draw in the fishing lines to help the animals catch the answers to their calculations. You could use the multiplication square to help you.

9 x 5

9 x 3

7 x 8

27

56

45

Practice for all the times tables

The animals are playing games at the Paradise Park fair. Work out their scores at each stall. You could use the blank pages at the back of the book to write each multiplying calculation.

The more you practise your times tables, the easier they get.

Each coconut you knock down scores 7.

I've knocked down 8!

I only knocked down 6 when I did it!

Hop's score

Pin's score

Even numbers score double.

8

3

6

12

Zeb's score

Wolfy's score

Draw a star next to the animal who has the highest score at the fair.

Times tables quiz

Find out how much you can remember about the 7, 9, 11 and 12 times tables by doing this quiz. Answers on page 26.

A. Can you help the animals with this matching game? Draw a loopy line to match each times table question to its correct answer in one of the circles.

77

108

7 × 11

72

72

108

12 × 9

8 × 9

6 × 12

9 × 12

B. Complete these times tables calculations for Pin and Wolfy.

7 x 6 = ☐

8 x 7 = ☐

8 x 12 = ☐

9 x 11 = ☐

12 x 7 = ☐

7 x 9 = ☐

10 x 11 = ☐

9 x 6 = ☐

7 x 3 = ☐

11 x 12 = ☐

7 x 12 = ☐

12 x 12 = ☐

Quiz answers

A.

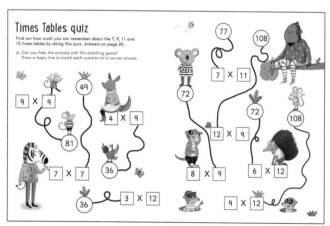

Times Tables quiz

Find out how much you can remember about the 7, 9, 11 and 12 times tables by doing this quiz. Answers on page 26.

A. Can you help the animals with this matching game? Draw a loopy line to match each question to its correct answer.

77 108
9 X 9
49
7 X 11
72
4 X 9
72
108
12 X 9
81
6 X 12
7 X 7 36
8 X 9
36 3 X 12
9 X 12

B.

7 x 6 = 42	10 x 11 = 110
8 x 7 = 56	9 x 6 = 54
8 x 12 = 96	7 x 3 = 21
9 x 11 = 99	11 x 12 = 132
12 x 7 = 84	7 x 12 = 84
7 x 9 = 63	12 x 12 = 144

There are two answer possibilities for 36, 72 and 108. You may have joined them up the other way to the answers shown here.

Score 1 point for each correct answer and write your score in this box: **21**

Answers

pages 4-5

$3 \times 6 = 18$

$3 \times 3 = 9$

$3 \times 8 = 24$

$3 \times 7 = 21$

$4 \times 10 = 40$

$4 \times 6 = 24$

$4 \times 9 = 36$

$4 \times 8 = 32$

$6 \times 6 = 36$

$6 \times 3 = 18$

$6 \times 8 = 48$

$6 \times 7 = 42$

$8 \times 10 = 80$

$8 \times 6 = 48$

$8 \times 9 = 72$

$8 \times 8 = 64$

pages 6-7

$4 \times 7 = 28$

$8 \times 7 = 56$

$1 \times 7 = 7$

$2 \times 7 = 14$

$3 \times 7 = 21$

$4 \times 7 = 28$

$5 \times 7 = 35$

$6 \times 7 = 42$

$7 \times 7 = 49$

$8 \times 7 = 56$

$9 \times 7 = 63$

$10 \times 7 = 70$

pages 8-9

$1 \times 9 = 9$

$2 \times 9 = 18$

$3 \times 9 = 27$

$4 \times 9 = 36$

$5 \times 9 = 45$

For further 9 times tables calculations, see answers for page 13.

pages 10-11

$1 \times 10 = 10$

$2 \times 10 = 20$

$3 \times 10 = 30$

$1 \times 11 = 11$

$2 \times 11 = 22$

$3 \times 11 = 33$

$4 \times 11 = 44$

$5 \times 11 = 55$

$1 \times 12 = 12$

$2 \times 12 = 24$

$3 \times 12 = 36$

page 12

99 is in both the 9 and 11 times tables.

page 13

$1 \times 9 = 9$

$2 \times 9 = 18$

$3 \times 9 = 27$

$4 \times 9 = 36$

$5 \times 9 = 45$

$6 \times 9 = 54$

$7 \times 9 = 63$

$8 \times 9 = 72$

$9 \times 9 = 81$

$10 \times 9 = 90$

$1 \times 11 = 11$

$2 \times 11 = 22$

$3 \times 11 = 33$

$4 \times 11 = 44$

$5 \times 11 = 55$

$6 \times 11 = 66$

$7 \times 11 = 77$

$8 \times 11 = 88$

$9 \times 11 = 99$

$10 \times 11 = 110$

pages 14-15

$4 \times 9 = 36$

$8 \times 11 = 88$

$9 \times 10 = 90$

$9 \times 11 = 99$

$5 \times 9 = 45$

$9 \times 9 = 81$

pages 16-17

1	2	3	4	5	6	7	8	9	10
11	(12)	13	14	15	16	17	18	19	20
21	22	23	(24)	25	26	27	28	29	30
31	32	33	34	35	(36)	37	38	39	40
41	42	43	44	45	46	47	(48)	49	50
51	52	53	54	55	56	57	58	59	(60)
61	62	63	64	65	66	67	68	69	70
71	(72)	73	74	75	76	77	78	79	80
81	82	83	(84)	85	86	87	88	89	90
91	92	93	94	95	(96)	97	98	99	100
101	102	103	104	105	106	107	(108)	109	110
111	112	113	114	115	116	117	118	119	(120)
121	122	123	124	125	126	127	128	129	130
131	(132)	133	134	135	136	137	138	139	140
141	142	143	(144)	145	146	147	148	149	150

$1 \times 12 = 12$

$2 \times 12 = 24$

$3 \times 12 = 36$

$4 \times 12 = 48$

$5 \times 12 = 60$

$6 \times 12 = 72$

$7 \times 12 = 84$

$8 \times 12 = 96$

$9 \times 12 = 108$

$10 \times 12 = 120$

$11 \times 12 = 132$

$12 \times 12 = 144$

pages 18-19

$7 \times 5 = 35$

$2 \times 12 = 24$

$7 \times 3 = 21$

$6 \times 12 = 72$

$12 \times 10 = 120$

$7 \times 7 = 49$

pages 20-21

$9 \times 5 = 45$ $9 \times 3 = 27$ $7 \times 8 = 56$

pages 22-23

Hop's score: 56 ★

Pin's score: 42

Zeb's score: 16

Wolfy's score: 24

Pat's score: 18

Gloria's score: 12

Kat's score: 6

Ping's score: 15

Bruce's score: 30

You can use these pages to practise writing your times tables.

My seeds come in packets of 9.

How many seeds would there be in 4 packets?

How many seeds would there be in 8 packets?

Remember, you could use the 10 times table to help you.

Do you know your
11 and **12** times tables?
Write all the calculations
you can remember
on this page.

Notes for grown-ups

Times tables reminder (pages 4-5)

Children may remember that multiplying calculations can be written either way around. For example, the answer to 4 x 10 is the same as for 10 x 4. This may help children if they feel more confident counting in 10s than 4s, or are more confident with some tables than others.

Groups of 7/The 7 times table (pages 6-7)

If children are confident with most other tables, they will already know many of the numbers in the 7 times table. For example, if they are confident with the 5 times table, then they will be able to write the answer for 5 x 7. You could encourage them to count forward and back in 7s.

Groups of 9 (pages 8-9)

The 9 times table can be difficult to remember, but the 10 times table is much easier. If children are confident with the 10 times table, they can find the answer as if it was a multiplication with 10 (instead of 9), then subtract the other number. For example, 10 x 5 = 50. 9 x 5 = 45. The difference is 5.

Groups of 11 (pages 10-11)

This activity allows children to see that the 11 times table has a clear pattern, like the 10 times table. You could encourage children to count in 11s as far as they can go, and back again. If children are confident, they could try writing 12 times table calculations, with 12 flags on each string.

The 9 and 11 times tables (pages 12-13)

Children may notice these patterns: the last digit in the numbers in the 9 times table decreases each time (9, 8, 7 etc.), while the last digit in numbers in the 11 times table increases each time (1, 2, 3 etc.).

Word problems for 9 and 11 (pages 14-15)

This activity tests children's recall of the 9 and 11 times tables. Support children in working out what the numbers to multiply together are, in each scenario. Remind them that the numbers can be written either way around in the calculation, which could help them if they are more confident with some tables than others.

The 12 times table (pages 16-17)

Children could practise doubling the numbers in the 6 times table and halving the numbers in the 12 times table.

Word problems for 7 and 12 (pages 18-19)

This activity tests children's recall of the trickier 7 and 12 times tables. Support children in working out what the numbers to multiply together are in each scenario. Remind them that the numbers can be written either way around in the calculation, which could help them if they are more confident with some tables than others.

Multiplication square (pages 20-21)

Help children, if necessary, with using the multiplication square to find the answer to any multiplication question.

Practice for all the times tables (pages 22-23)

This is a test of children's recall of all the times tables they have learned. Support children in working out what the numbers to multiply together are, for each animal's score.